# 7 Steps t Overcoming Bullying

D1409611

## (An Awareness Guide.)

By
Tiffany "Mikki High" Hoffman

## Seven Steps to Overcoming Bullying

© 2021 Tiffany M. Hoffman

Published by AMC Consultants

Tiffany M. Hoffman

Disclaimer:

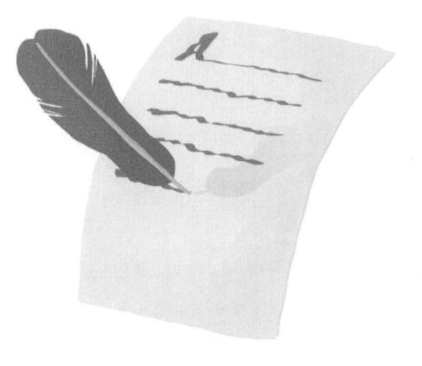

## Abstract

Bullying is an issue that has plagued our society for many years. Through my years of study, I have learned that when this issue is addressed properly; there is a lessened risk of lives being lost. I have seen many instances when this situation was not

properly dealt with and many individuals were affected negatively. In my opinion, this epidemic of bullying does not have to be! This document intends to equip individuals and groups with tools and methods that enable them to be successful on their journey to overcoming bullying. Throughout this series, a plethora of questions will be answered: a) What is Bullying? b) What are the methods to overcome bullying? c) What are examples of individuals that have overcome this issue?

# Dedication

*This book is dedicated to my father, mother, and all those who have been bullied. Know that you are not alone.*

# Introduction

Several steps can assist an individual with their journey to overcoming bullying. In this work, there is an intention to bring awareness to these solutions. Furthermore, my goal is to shed a light of hope for individuals that are desperately in need of resources! In addition, there is a desire is to help save the lives of those that feel they cannot endure life any longer under such harsh victimization. This awareness guide is intended to aid them in their triumph over their specific situation of bullying. Although bullying circumstances vary, some steps can be established to assist with this overall goal of being aware of the cause of and solution to bullying.

Throughout my life and career, I have encountered countless cases of young people and adults facing the turmoil of bullying in their own lives. This has honestly caused me to want to make a difference. Although bullying is an unfortunate component in our society that has occurred for years, I do believe that if we become aware of the cause of and solution to this issue (*even if it is one person at a time*), that we can stamp it out together!

"Never allow the pain of your past to hinder you from the opportunities of your future."

-Tiffany "Mikki High" Hoffman

# Table of Contents

# **Table of Contents**

# Table of Contents

Your S.H.A.P.E

# Chapter One- Step 1: Understand/Accept Your S.H.A.P.E.

### *Part A: Understand Your Shape*

Several measures can be taken to overcoming bullying. The goal of this awareness guide is to simply share with you some of the measures that researchers have found effective. I have also incorporated elements that have been key to helping me to overcome bullying in my own life. **The first step** that I am going to share with you is one that is truly dear to my heart. I have decided to align this initial component as the first step simply because it is the foundation of the steps that I will discuss with you later.

So, the first foundational implementation which has

assisted many people with overcoming bullying has been to understand their S.H.A.P.E. It is essential to note that one may never fully grasp understanding, acceptance, or love from other individuals until understanding, accepting, and loving themselves. Research reveals that bullies are known to target those that they believe can be easily overthrown. Often, bullies prey on individuals who are different than everyone else. People tend to wonder why an individual would do such a thing. Many times, the bullies have trauma in their own lives. So, some tend to intimidate those that could enable them to feel more in control or superior over their circumstances.

A recent study reveals that bullies regularly target

individuals that stand out among the crowd.

It also seems as though they target individuals that are struggling to analyze the way that they mesh into the environment surrounding them.

There are many instances where students naturally stand out. Maybe their intelligence, weight, race, or social status varies from the norm of the crowd. This could easily cause a particular student to be a target for bullying. Certain steps, however, can be implemented to help targeted students. The simple truth is that many cases involve fearful bullies. They are simply afraid that a particular individual with unique qualities may outshine the similarities that take place.

among the common crowd.

By opinion, sometimes it is not necessarily better to fit in; sometimes an individual is meant to stand out. This is one of the primary reasons why the first step to overcoming bullying is to understand your SHAPE! At first glance, it may seem that this statement is about an individual loving their own body shape. Although one should; this statement goes much deeper than the outer appearance. Individuals need to have a clear understanding of who they are on the inside because quite frequently this affects the way that individuals portray themselves on the outside. When children are young their guardian(s) are noted as being the key component to helping them decipher who they are.

My father would always tell my siblings and me "get a sheet of paper and jot down the letters S.H.A.P.E, one on top of the other".

He asked us to take a moment and think about "S". He would ask, "What are your spiritual gifts?". These are qualities that are given to you on the inside which come out on the outside to help you and others. For instance, some are natural-born leaders, while others are excellent at assisting. When you take a moment to find out your spiritual gifts; you begin to understand, accept, and love who you are!

The next letter that we would jot down was "H"; This stands for the heart's desire.

The next step to understanding yourself is to ask the following question: What is it that I have a passion to accomplish? In other words, what do I love to do? Some people have a heart's desire to help animals, while some have a

heart's desire for young people.

There are so many desires that people have in their heart to accomplish. This list is so vast that one can narrow their true heart's desire down by using the following step.

"A" stands for abilities. Many people want to do something; however, it may not be the time. Thus, when analyzing your heart's desire, it is helpful to also analyze what

you are *good* at doing. There are countless abilities in the world. Some are good at speaking, programming, writing, sketching, singing, playing instruments, etc. Just be sure that you are honing your own and not someone else's.

Now, the next letter that we will observe is "P". This letter stands for personality. Yes, some may have a heart's desire to be a waitress. They may know how to move the tables and hold multiple plates, but their personality is wrong for that environment.

My father would always say "This is how you get nurses with a traffic director attitude". So, it is important to make sure that all the other components mentioned above line up with your personality.

The final letter in step one of overcoming the issue of bullying is "E" which represents experience. Yes, you may have a heart's desire to save the animals, teach kids, or even be a waitress; but do you have the experience to do so. This is where education plays a huge part. If you do not have experience in the area you would like to be a part of- do not sweat, it…get it. Find a way to gain *experience* for your passion; it will only make you better!

Having this understanding helped me so much throughout my childhood. Honestly, it still helps me even in my adulthood today. Knowing who you are is essential to know where you are going. This reminds me of one of my favorite verses of scripture in Proverbs 29:18.

*"Where there is no vision, the people perish: but he that keepeth the law, happy is he.".*

To me, this can be translated as…. if you have some idea of where you are headed then you will be happier, as opposed to trying to move forward with no vision, foresight, or forethought.

Steps like this first one have been a key element of my triumph over bullying. Hopefully, you or someone that you know will find these principles helpful. I can remember many times when I felt unsure as a child and I was able to refer to the advice and encouragement of my parents. They would say things like… "Remember, you have a special S.H.A.P.E" or "Don't worry God has a special plan for your life".

Motivational Moment:
"Don't let others stop you from being who you are. Don't let other children's opinions stop you from being who God made you to be."
-Grace, Bully No More Partner

Through times of being bullied; it is encouraging moments and words like this that are ever so important to the development of an individual.

Understanding your make- up is one thing; however, learning to accept it can be a totally different venture. This brings me to the next element of our discussion.

> *Stat: There are about 282,000 students that are reportedly attacked in high schools throughout the nation each month.*

# *Part B: Accept your S.H.A.P.E.*

Quite often individuals will have a perfectly good S.H.A.P.E, but because they do not understand it- they fight the process of accepting it. In some instances, this occurs when an individual is deeply tuned into the S.H.A.P.E of another. Unfortunately, instead of discovering their own gifts, passions, talents, and abilities; some individuals tend to have a desire to embody someone else's. This desire is what causes a plethora of people to get off track. Statistics state that only three percent of college graduates work in the field that they obtained a degree.

This does not mean that people should not strive to get an education. This can however mean that it is so important for an individual to begin understanding who they are from an early age.

This helps to cause an assurance rather than a future weakness. Once an individual gains an understanding of their passion and puts it into practice there is usually little to no trouble with accepting who they are.

People frequently have insecurities because they do not understand who they are. Once an individual has learned this, it is then vital to come to grips with their natural S.H.A.P.E rather than try and alter it to fit into a certain clique. This type of thinking could cause a student to forfeit the great accomplishments that they could otherwise achieve.

It is quite funny, because oftentimes a child may not be able to see who they are on their own. So, research reveals that many times they tend to mold to the shape of those around them.

During times like this, it has been deemed important to have them surrounded by those that are of a positive reinforcement.

Before continuing in our detailed journey of understanding elements that help overcome bullying; One of the many stories that I have come across when assisting with raising awareness to such a heart-wrenching cause over the years. The story that I want to share with you is about a young girl who faced bullying at a very early age in her own life.

*Stat: A reported 15% of all students who do not show up for school report it to be out of fear of being bullied.*

The following is a real-life example of a young girl who was bullied and spoke out about her situation. For confidentiality purposes, the name has been altered to Izzy. Also, due to grammar errors, this story has been edited.

## Storytime: Izzy

Izzy shared how when she was in the fifth grade that she did not know very many people. Other children did not want to be around her because she failed the fifth grade, and most people knew about it. Her classmates thought that it was funny to verbally bully her by calling her a "loser" or "failure

in life". Izzy said that these children said many other mean things to her, but she tried her best not to care about it. Sadly, the children became more determined and comfortable with harassing Izzy. These same children that were verbally bullying her now began to not only call her names, but they began to do things like pushing and shoving her.

As Izzy grew older, she became a bit more "popular". She stated that it was not because she chose to follow the bullying cycle and become a bully herself. It was not even because she became the captain of the cheerleading squad.

She did not like sports very much at all. Izzy gained her popularity and respect from others through simple acts of kindness. She chose to do her best to give other children good advice and do kind things for them. This

was refreshing to many students due to the horrendous environment of bullying which otherwise surrounded them.

As time went on, there was one girl in particular who thought that it would be exciting if she targeted Izzy to make her life miserable.

To accomplish this goal, the bullying girl spread many rumors about Izzy. She also decided to take the time to write threats down in the girl's restroom which were directed at Izzy. The bully would write statements saying that she would physically harm her. Although she never did much physical damage other than pushing and verbally harassing her; the threats were frightening enough to cause Izzy to fall into a

deep depression.

She began self-harming acts such as cutting. Sadly, she thought that if she could hurt herself physically… maybe the mental and

emotional pain would go away. As bullying does with many

students, this caused Izzy to have a huge desire for her

schooling to be over. She desperately desired to move to the

ninth grade in order to get a fresh start.

Izzy began the ninth grade, but still had not fully dealt with the mental trauma that she faced from bullying in her previous grade level. So, as she progressed to the ninth grade,  she faced some of the same circumstances and fears. Not only did she face fear and depression, but she even began to have signs of anxiety and suicidal thoughts.

*Stat: According to a SAFE survey, teens in grades 6-10, are the most likely to be involved in bullying activities*

It had begun to get to the point where she had no desire to be a part of her English class.

This was mostly because this is where much of her bullying occurred. So, Izzy would run to her friend's session and explain to her that she did not want to be a part of her current class.

Motivational Moment:
"Keep pushing! All those who harm you are afraid of their own insecurities."
-Katoria, Bully No More Partner

It was at this time that Izzy's friend looked her in the eyes with conviction. She told her that even though she may not be able to do very much that she is willing to be there for her when she needs to talk. Once Izzy spoke with her friend, she decided to share her circumstances with a trusted counselor.

Her only request was that her friend is willing to go with her.

Stat: About 42% of kids have been bullied while online with one in four being verbally attacked more than once.

Once Izzy chose to implement this level of communication, she found that the problem stopped. Izzy expressed immense thanks to her friend and God for giving her strength through trying circumstances at an early age.

Izzy has now given her life to God and has found peace in giving Him all her issues.

She says that He has set her free from depression, anxiety, suicidal tendencies, and each of the other problems that she was facing. Finally, the scars that she has, she wears them as a testimony and encouragement to others proving that bullying can be overcome!

# Summary/ Key Takeaways: Step 1

- It is essential to note that one may never fully grasp understanding, acceptance, or love from other individuals until understanding, accepting, and loving themselves.

- Many times, the bullies have trauma in their own lives.

- Bullies regularly target individuals that stand out among the crowd.

- Statistics state that only three percent of college graduates work in the field that they obtained a degree.

- It is so important for an individual to begin understanding who they are from an early age.

- *Stat: According to a SAFE survey, teens in grades 6-10, are the most likely to be involved in bullying activities*

In the next chapter, you will learn about the importance of understanding what bullying is. There will also be a discussion of what bullying is not.

# Step Two:

# Know
## What Bullying Is

## Chapter Two- Step 2: Know What Bullying Is

The **second step** that is necessary in

order to overcome is to have a clear understanding of what

bullying is and what bullying is not. Many people in society

have their own opinion of what bullying is; however,

researchers have outlined a general idea about how bullying

can be defined. Bullying is primarily viewed as ***unwanted***

***aggressive behavior.***

Stat: Other recent bullying statistics reveal that 54% of students reported that witnessing physical abuse at home can lead to violence at school.

This term is often used to describe harassment that affects those in school; however, it extends far beyond this scenario! It usually refers to an action that is intentional and involves an imbalance of strength or even power.

If not corrected, this behavior typically continues over an extended period.

Other components that indicate that a particular circumstance is bullying are as follows:

- A particular individual is continually targeted.

- An individual or group of individuals have the intention of hurting, embarrassing or intimidating a particular individual in one way or another.

- The negative encounters that come about are deemed as a true imbalance of power and/or strength.

For instance, the person that is considered the bully is stronger than the victim or maybe even more popular. It is also vital to recall that each situation of unwanted aggressive behavior is different. There is not necessarily a cookie cut way to handle all bullying.

*Stat: Some of the top years for bullying include 4$^{th}$ through 8$^{th}$ graders in which about 90% were reported as victims of bullying.*

However, the steps in this guide can assist an individual

in their journey to freedom.

Motivational Moment:
"DON'T LET THEM BRING YOU DOWN YOU ARE STRONG!
                    -Jenascia, Bully No More Partner

# Summary/ Key Takeaways: Step 2

- Bullying is primarily viewed as ***unwanted aggressive behavior.***

- Each situation of unwanted aggressive behavior is different.

- There are key elements that can help identify if an individual is truly bullied.

- *Other recent bullying statistics reveal that 54% of students reported that witnessing physical abuse at home can lead to violence at school.*

In the next chapter, you will learn to analyze a bullying circumstance.

## Step Three: Analyze Your Situation

Analyzing a bullying circumstance is the **third step** in safely deflating such an issue. Analyzing may seem like a bit of a journey, but it has been found to help individuals implement the correct measures to overcoming bullying.

It also helps to make sure that the appropriate measures are being taken. In other words, analyzing can help to guide a parent, student, teacher, or guardian to the appropriate response rather than reaction.

Before we continue with components of analyzing; let us further observe reaction versus responding. Firstly, many individuals tend to use the terms interchangeably.

However, psychologists have found that the two terms have drastic variations in definition. A reaction is usually done quickly and with little to no thought. It is also done with some sort of aggression and tension. Furthermore,

when an individual reacts it tends to attract more reactions. This allows a person to see that reaction may not be the best route to take. If the desire is to safely deflate a bullying circumstance, the response should be encouraged. In most cases, it rather fuels this type of scenario to continue.

On the other hand, a response is well thought out and usually results in the safe resolution of a circumstance of violence. It is also a good idea to note that a response is calm and tends to provide a resolution that is non-threatening.

First, there must be a clear understanding of who the victim is. A question to ask yourself when analyzing this would be: Who is the true person being attacked, intimidated, or embarrassed?

Some indications that an individual is a victim in a certain scenario as follows:

- Coming home with bruises, cuts, or other injuries that are not usually explained.

- Indications of damaged possessions (i.e., clothes, shoes, class materials)

- Lost items

- Frequent complaints of sickness before school

- Skipping classes

- Tactics were implemented to avoid attending school.

- Tactics were implemented to avoid a certain route to school.

- Disinterest in riding the school bus.

- Acting depressed

- Acting sad

- Social withdrawal

- Stating the feeling of being picked on.

- Visible low self-esteem

- Mood swings (i.e., one moment angry than sad)

- Wanting to run away.

- Interest in taking a weapon to school.

- Suicidal tendencies

- Discussing being violent to others

Secondly, there must be a clear understanding of who the bully is in question. There are a lot of characteristics that make up a bully. It is important to know these components so that the wrong individual does not face negative repercussions. One thing that is important to note about a bully is that they do not choose to take responsibility for their actions. Lots of times, they may even try to frame the victim as the cause of the bullying.

This is usually done by choosing a target that has had issues with things like lying and troublemaking in the past.

Some signs of a bully are as follows:

The individual gets into physical or verbal altercations.

- The harasser, in question, has friends that practice bullying other individuals.

- Their aggression consistently increases.

- They are constantly being sent to disciplinary authority figures such as the principal.

- Another sign is that the bully continues to obtain new items without truthful explanations.

They may be obtaining items such as clothes, finances, food, or even various supplies. An additional sign of a bully is that they try to place the blame for their problems on other people. Additionally, bullies tend to be competitive. They also stress about their status, reputation, or popularity.

Individuals may have a lot of excuses for why they choose to bully. For example, they may want to fit in as stated earlier. They may even simply want more control over other people. It is known that those who bully usually choose those

who they believe to be physically or mentally weaker than they are. Many times, physical bullies use tactics of intimidation such as hanging out with peers that encourage their abusive behavior. Bullies usually have issues with the following:

- Self-Control

- Obeying Rules

- Compassion (caring for other people)

These same bullies have a high-risk factor which increases the chance that they will have issues later in life as well. Some of these issues are as follows:

- Violence

- Criminal Behavior

- Failed Relationships

- Failed Career(s)

As stated earlier, bullies often target victims who they deem to be weaker than themselves. They may also target those who they see as being socially marginalized for one reason or another. Some of these reasons are as follows:

- Weight

- Ethnicity

- Disabilities

- Intellect

- Other characteristics that may cause an individual to stand out or appear unique.

Unfortunately, oftentimes the issue of bullying tends to result in major consequences for the victim. Some of these negative effects are as follows:

- Low self-esteem

- Depression

- School trouble

- Violent behavior

Parents or guardians must be able to recognize signs that physical bullying is occurring. Recognizing these signs could help prevent the bully-victim from suffering for a prolonged period.

If a child happens to be victimized by bullies, those around them must show them as much love and compassion as possible. It is also vital that the victim is aware of the fact that it is not their fault. Furthermore, having conversations with the individual being victimized to gain an understanding of the way that bullying is happening is also very important.

Secondly, it is essential that once such information is gathered that it is reported to an authority figure such as a teacher or school administrator.

Each bullying situation should be taken seriously. There should always be an effort to find the best solution to the variations of circumstances that may occur.

*Stat: There are about 71% of students that report bullying as an ongoing problem.*

One of the basic solutions that have worked for many young people is to ignore the bully. In other circumstances, they chose to stay near friends or adult supervision to avoid being bullied.

Another avenue that has worked for many people has been to speak with a counselor about what they have been going through; Especially if they have been facing elements of anger or depression. These are only a few solutions that have assisted individuals.

However, we will discuss many of these in greater detail later in this guide. On the other hand of the spectrum if an individual is a bully; it is important to make it clear to them that such behavior is not be allowed.

Researchers state that it is also helpful for parents to have regular conversations with their children about the things that occur throughout their day. It is also believed that parents should make it clear to their children that they should in no way support bullying.

> *Fact: Mean hurtful comments, and spreading rumors are the most common types of cyberbullying.*

Many also believe that it is vital for authority figures to heighten anti-bullying measures, such as anti-bullying campaigns, supervision, zero-tolerance policies, and even various types of counseling. Furthermore, there should be an understanding of which method of bullying is being used. Finally, it is helpful to research such aspects as a locale in which the situations of harassment occur.

Research reveals that bullying has shown its face in many forms throughout our society.

Some variations or methods of bullying are as follows:

- Hitting/Punching

- Kicking

- Teasing/ Name

  Calling

- Rumors

- Social exclusion

- Technological abuse

Each of the above actions belongs to a particular category of bullying. In the next part of our discussion, there will be a description of the four most common forms of bullying. Having an understanding of the category of bullying is a component that could be helpful to an individual being victimized by such taunts.

## *Part A: Physical Bullying*

The first category of bullying that we will cover is physical bullying. Physical bullying is a very serious form of bullying that affects more than the victim. This type of abuse affects the bully, the victim, and bystanders who view it. It is also considered one of the easiest methods of bullying to spot. Students and authority figures (i.e., parents, teachers, principals) should be aware of what is constituted as physical bullying. They should also be aware of some implementations that can be used to handle it.

Many negative actions constitute physical bullying. Some of these negative interactions that may come about are as follows:

- Hitting/Punching

- Kicking

- Shoving

- Fighting

- Practical Jokes

- Stealing

- Destroying

  belongings

- Sexual harassment

- Tripping

- Slapping

- Spitting

*Again, for the previous actions to be in the category of bullying the following must also be true:*

- A particular individual is continually targeted.

- An individual or group of individuals have the intention of hurting, embarrassing or intimidating a particular person in one way or another.

- The negative encounters that come about are deemed as a true imbalance of power and/or strength. For instance, the person that is considered the bully is stronger than the victim or maybe even more popular.

Research reveals that physical bullying is evident  primarily at school. It is also important to note that it is possible for physical bullying to happen after school or off school grounds. It has been found that bullying is most common in middle school.

Surveys have revealed that nearly all middle school students have been directly or indirectly affected by bullying in some way. Oftentimes, at this stage, individuals have a desire to fit in with their peers. This usually leads to students engaging in acts of bullying. Many times, those that choose NOT to engage in these acts of bullying stand out and are targeted by those who bully.

Although bullying is very prevalent in middle school; it is also visible in earlier grade levels and high school. If the situation is not corrected it even continues into adulthood. Previously, physical bullying is more common among males.

Although the previous statement is true, it is vital to remember that females also physically bully.

## *Part B- Cyberbullying:*

Technology has developed multiple windows for

 bullying to occur. Some examples being the implementation of email systems, instant messaging, websites, calling systems, and even text messaging.

The use of technology for bullying is called cyberbullying.

Today, this form of bullying has become quite prevalent. This

method of bullying is used by children and adults.

*Stat: Over 80% of these teens use a cell phone regularly, making it the most popular form of technology and a common tool for cyberbullying.*

Some choose technology to bully because it allows them to reach many people and obscure their identity. This form of bullying must be addressed; especially when noting that individuals are online at least three hours a day and are on their cell phones approximately eighty percent of the time.

Also, about half of young people have experienced some form of cyberbullying, and 10 to 20 percent experience it regularly. Research also proves that mean, hurtful comments, and spreading rumors are the most common type of cyberbullying.

One major thing to remember about cyberbullying is – you have the power! have the power! Several measures can be made to help an individual solve the circumstance of cyberbullying. The first thing is: If the cyber offense is serious enough; it could be charged as a criminal activity. For example, An individual's passwords were hacked or if any threats were made. These actions would be grounds for an individual to be charged as a delinquent under the law.

Also, when cyberbullying becomes too much to handle- shut it off until you have the strength to deal with the situation.

Minimizing the time spent online and on devices such   as cell

phones and computers have been effective methods of therapy

for many individuals facing cyberbullying. Also, if an

individual is cyberbullied the following steps have also

proven to be effective. One of the first things to do if you are

bullied online would be to take note of who is bullying you

online.

A great way to do this is to find out which account the bullying is coming from. Also, take note of the exact harmful communication that took place. Take note of the time that the bullying happened. What is the name of the individual that said it? You should also keep an adequate record for the  sake of proof. Another tip would be that if you are being bullied...handle this situation with a parent or guardian.

It can be very difficult to face any type of bullying alone…let alone cyberbullying. One very effective way to apply these tips is to take a screenshot and be sure to include all the information that was outlined above. Once this is done report the incident along with the evidence. Furthermore, most social media platforms have a method to report such incidents. They also usually have policies and procedures that show that they stand against bullying.

When a person signs up for the account it means that they submit or agree to the policies and procedures.

Furthermore, an application that may help an individual in their journey to preventing cyberbullying is for the parent or guardian to monitor the online activity of the child. Some individuals wonder how to monitor a young one's online activity. Here are some tips that may be helpful with monitoring: One, use the apps that are identical to the ones that the child is using. Doing so will be essential in helping the authority figure to comprehend what the young one is doing in cyberspace.

This will help to provide direction as far as what the application entails. It will often unveil the potential hazards of the application. Searching terms such as usage, privacy, reviews, and risks can help provide much of the information concerning the application.

Another great tip is communicating with your children about online safety and the risks of online bullying. Talk to them concerning what they  take part in online. It is a good idea for these conversations to be done regularly rather than sporadic. The fourth helpful component is recognizing rules and regulations for internet usage.

Most social media platforms include information that assists parents or guardians with boundaries for online or social media usage. Some platforms even include contracts for parents and their young ones. Such a contract helps provide an outline that the parent can use, and the child can follow. This is also a method of developing an agreement that the

child must follow. The final component that is suggested to assist with protecting a child online would be to follow the age restrictions that are provided on the various platforms and devices that they desire to acquire.

> **Bonus Tip!** *Block interaction with cyberbullies from all technological and social media platforms.*

Most circumstances of cyberbullying that occur among young children can be avoided by simply following the age restrictions that are provided.

It is also vital to share any information that you acquire concerning bullies online with those that you interact with online as well.

## *Part C- Verbal Bullying*

Verbal bullying can be simply defined as bullying that is done through words. Whether writing or speaking. Some examples are as follows:

- Insults

- Teasing

- Etc.

Verbal bullying is done to gain power over an individual's

peers through this form of intimidation. This form of bullying can be extremely damaging to the victim. It could be so detrimental that the victim may even suffer psychological effects. Research reveals that this form of bullying is most common among girls.

Motivational Moment:
"No matter what any person says negatively to you or about you; just know that you are somebody important."
-Sarah, Bully No More Partner

## *Part D- Social Bullying:*

Social bullying is also known as relational bullying. This is known as one of the most common among girls and usually circulates around an individual trying to hurt their peer. It can even occur because of a particular peer's standing within a certain group. Relational or Social bullying can be used as a method to allow bullies to advance their standing in their social setting and control others.

Sometimes social bullying can be one of the hardest variations of bullying to detect. This is simply because it is not as overt as an issue such as physical bullying.

While various forms of harassment happen in our society; the term bullying primarily applies to those that are students. This is quite apparent when comprehending the fact that many startling statistics unveil the  severity of bullying. One major statistic within the United States is that over one hundred and sixty thousand students avoid school each day for fear that they would be bullied. In my opinion, this statistic alone should enable an individual to see that positive action needs to be taken to raise awareness of this issue called bullying.

In the following segments of this document, there will be steps presented to assist a student that is struggling with gaining leverage over the circumstance of school harassment. Later, there will be a description of areas where bullying occurs in school. Although the terms vary it is important to

recall that unwanted aggressive behavior does not only happen in schools, nor does it only happen to children. This type of behavior has also been known to occur off school grounds. For instance, this can also happen at home.

Siblings have been noted to bully each other on many occasions. Bullying also happens among adults as well. Yes, usually a term such as "harassment" is used when referring to bullying that pertains to adults; but it is still the same type of behavior.

## *Part E- Workplace Bullying:*

One area where adult bullying is prevalent is in the  workplace. On various occasions, there have been notations of adults who treat their co-workers with little respect. There have also been accounts of employees who purposely sabotaged the assignments of their co-workers. Adults with the mindset of a bully tend to consistently criticize their targets even if it is unwelcomed. They will even try and make the accomplishments of their targets seem as if they are insignificant. Another way that adults have been recorded to bully is by filing false claims of grievances that are in their favor. This type of behavior occurs frequently because the individual views their target as a threat to their position of power. They may be fearful of losing their job and rather than improving performance; they choose the route of shattering their co-worker's reputation. On the other hand, some adults bully simply because they are jealous of the influence of another employee. It is vital for an individual in this situation to remember that they have a way out.

One of my favorite scriptures...Deuteronomy 28:7 says,

"The Lord shall cause thine enemies that rise against thee to be smitten before thy face: they shall come out against thee one way and flee before thee seven ways."

*Part F: How to Solve*

1) Keep a private record- this helps you to remember when and why you felt bullied. It is a good idea to keep records of the date/time, who the bully is, the bully's exact actions, the location it occurs, a witness, and how it affects you.

2) Check for an official bully policy for your workplace.

3) Set up a meeting with your manager.

4) Have a talk with HR about your situation. If the bullying continues after you have exhausted all means within the organization, then it is necessary to follow the next step.

5) Contact an external source- this could be your state inspector, the fair work commission, or maybe even your union if you are a union member.

## Summary/ Key Takeaways: Step 3

- A reaction is usually done quickly and with little thought.

- A response is well thought out and usually results in the safe resolution of a circumstance of violence.

- There are signs which can help to identify a bully.

- Researchers state that it is also helpful for parents to have regular conversations with their children about the things that occur throughout their day.

- It is helpful to research such aspects as a locale in which the situations of harassment occur.

- There are many variations of bullying.

- *Stat: Over 80% of these teens use a cell phone regularly, making it the most popular form of technology and a common tool for cyberbullying.*

In the next chapter, you will learn how to build complementary relationships.

# Step Four:

# Build Complementary Relationships

# Chapter Four- Step 4:

# Build Complementary Relationships

The above point brings us to the **fourth step** highlighted in the resources of overcoming bullying- Build Complementary Relationships. When you build upon someone else's shape, you may attract the wrong relationships. Thus, once the individual has a clear understanding of who they are then they can begin to build complementary relationships.

People tend to be attracted to qualities such as personality and experience.

Once you build these relationships that compliment who you are then you can further advance in your mission to overcoming bullying. It is a known fact that bullies are attracted to those who are alone. Thus, one of the simplest ways to overcome this is by well…**not being alone!**

One system that my siblings and I always tried to implement was the "buddy system". This system is when a child is paired with at least one other child. The child that they are paired with is usually older and has more heightened instincts and abilities. This system is beneficial in assisting with things such as security, friendship, social necessities, problem-solving, and loneliness.

The buddy system is also proven to cause students to have an increased sense of belonging. It is also known to cause a greater feeling of inclusiveness in the school community. As a child, this system kept me from danger on countless occasions.

Furthermore, it is a good idea to understand where bullying occurs; this way proper precautions can be taken in helping to prevent bullying from happening. When speaking of school bullying; research also reveals that bullying is more

likely to occur in areas with poor or zero adult supervision. Research reveals that young boys tend to physically bully one another; While girls tend to use verbal bullying. Girls tend to do things such as using harsh words or spread rumors about one another.

Some areas to look out for bullying and use the buddy system are locations such as a) The playground. In primary school, bullying often occurs on the playground.

There are several places on playgrounds where students can easily hide and be obscured from adult supervision. This type of setup tends to lead to an environment that is realized as conducive to bullying. Another area that is recognized as a prevalent place that bullying occurs is b) The classroom.

Classroom bullying has proven to be more apparent among secondary level students.

Although in this environment an adult is usually present; students at this level find clever ways to subtly bully each other. Thus, things such as passing notes and making negative gestures are courses of action to look out for on the secondary level and sometimes on the primary level of schooling.

c)Finally, it has been found that bullying happens in-between classes. This negative behavior is prevalent in areas such as restrooms, lockers, and other areas such as changing rooms or even dormitories. So, in instances such as this, the buddy system is quite effective.

Several characteristics define an appropriate individual

to be a part of a child's buddy system. Firstly, the potential buddy must have a well-rounded understanding of their environment. Secondly, they must have a desire to be a positive mentor. The individual that is a potential buddy must also depict strong past performance in various aspects of school and relationships. They should have plenty of free time available for the individual they are to be in the buddy system with. It has also been proven helpful when the student chooses a buddy that is considered a peer. This peer should have good communication skills. It is also helpful if the "buddy to be" is respected among other students. These components should help in aiding an individual to properly gauge those who they can trust as official buddies in their "buddy system".

# Summary/ Key Takeaways: Step 4

- People tend to be attracted to qualities such as personality and experience.

- The buddy system is when a child is paired with at least one other child.

- There are many areas where bullies tend to lurk.

- Certain characteristics are necessary to be an effective "buddy".

In the next chapter, you will learn various methods of defense.

# Step Five:

# Build A Defense

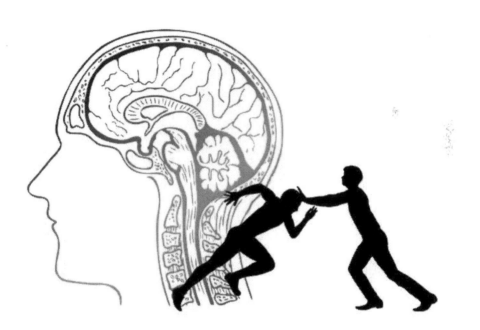

# Chapter 5- Step Five: Build A Defense

Once the situation is analyzed then the individual can

begin to build a defense. There are several methods concerning what is considered to be the proper defense for an individual dealing

with the issue of bullying. It is up to the individuals involved to decide on the most befitting measure of defense for their situation. The first method of defense is to have an adult to get involved. There are quite a few ways to do so. One way would be to make sure that the parent or guardian is aware of the harassment that has occurred. This is a beneficial measure to take simply because parents or guardians can be vocal on an adult level. For instance, they could express concern to teachers and others that are involved with the care of students

in the school system. Another benefit of getting a parent or

guardian involved in the fact that they may be able to end the

bullying situation by simply having a conversation with the

parent or guardian of the bully. A second way to get an adult

involved would be for the offended party to approach a school

authority themselves and express their concerns. Sometimes it

is easiest for the victim to reach out to a teacher that they feel

they can trust. Others find it more effective to reach out to an administrator or counselor. If this measure of defense is not effective; there may be a need for other safety measures.

A second method that has been effective in building a defense against bullies is for the offended party to assert themselves. One major factor is for the offended party to leave being a victim in their past. Even though the individual

may have been a victim, they do not need to continue to play this role.

Remaining the victim only tends to cause the bully to feel as though they have more power over the individual. It is helpful that a previous victim learns to carry their posture in a way that depicts confidence. A simple measure such as holding their head up is a way to show confidence. This type of

posture lessens the chances of the individual appearing weak.

Another method of assertion is the use of avoidance.

It is also very helpful to be cautious of students that tend to be troublesome. Avoidance tactics such as sitting near an adult, whether it be the bus driver, teacher, or other. Also, students can avoid bullying instances by carefully choosing their route to and from classes. Many students have also found it effective to avoid areas of the school that will be unsupervised; especially when the potential victim is alone.

Finally, if necessary, leave costly items and excess cash in a safe place. This should be done rather than walking around with such flashy materials. Doing the opposite of this may cause unnecessary conflict. Third, some individuals find it effective to bring a friend along as a source of strength. If avoidance  is not a possibility; it may be helpful to bring a buddy along to encourage the previous victim to be bold and either assert against the bully or find the meekness to ignore their harassment.

One major assertion technique has been for individuals to defend themselves verbally. Some take the route of either  being extremely calm, very nice, or even very strong in their speech. A final method of verbal defense that has been effective is humor. Either way, the primary purpose of verbal defense is to demonstrate that the individual is not afraid of the bully. Usually when a bully realizes that their tactics do not frighten the individual their sense of power is lost, and they leave the previous victim alone.

Another defense mechanism against bullies is of course- self-defense. Implementing lessons of general self-defense can be very beneficial in assisting a student with protecting themselves in a skillful manner. It also enables them to be alert to areas that are deemed unsafe.

Another excellent implementation is exercise and sports training. These tools can cause an individual to exude confidence which tends to discourage the attention of bullies.

Furthermore, if bullies still tend to try and bother the

individual; it is also effective to just simply walk away. An

 important factor of

walking away is to be

sure that the victim does

not appear afraid. It is

best to walk away with

an attitude that exudes

confidence. The final

implementation of self-

defense that can be

applied is the use of physical assertion against the bully. This

measure should only be used in cases where the student is in a

situation where there is no other way to protect themselves

against the bully.

The final method of defense against bullies that will be covered may seem unusual. Sometimes the best defense against a bully is to understand them. The first thing to note

about a bully is that they feed on power. Bullying is an instance that occurs because of a power imbalance. It is important to learn how to handle bullies at an early age; simply because bullying also occurs in adulthood. Gaining a clear understanding of this type of mindset without falling into the cycle of such behavior will also be a valuable tool

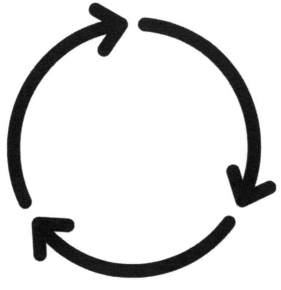

later in life. Another thing that may help someone deal with a bully is remembering that quite frequently, bullies are victims themselves.

Sometimes it is not a personal vendetta against a certain individual; it is simply a cry out for help. So, sometimes having a simple caring conversation with a bully can cause a positive change in events.

Before progressing in our discussion, I would like to share a story with you. The following story is a real-life example. The name has been altered to Matthew for confidentiality purposes.

## Storytime: Matthew

**Matthew's Story**:

Another story that I want to share with you is about a young boy who faced bullying in his own life. Matthew's father is active in the military and was actually deployed for a

large summation of his time as a child. He expressed that he and his family moved quite a lot. At one point they were moving approximately every two to three years. Matthew stated that due to moving so much; it was harder to make friends. Many of his classmates felt that because he was the "new kid" he would be an easy target to bully.

Matthew shared that he was bullied for any reason that the bullies could think of. A few target points that they directed their torment at was that, in the third grade, he stood out from among the crowd. Most of the time bullies targeted him because he was small, thin, had larger facial features, a high-pitched voice, and a military backpack.

They of course targeted him for other reasons, but these are the primary areas that offended Matthew.

Matthew stated in so many words that it was difficult to enjoy life. He also expressed that at an early age he wanted to give up on living. He said that because of bullying he cried every single day. He also tried to do everything that he could to blend in. He thought that if he laid low or hid that he could

avoid being bullied. He also tried playing contact sports such as football, but this only resulted in him obtaining a concussion. Matthew believes that this concussion came about because the coach decided to put him, weighing only 87 pounds as a freshman, against a nearly 300-pound freshman at fullback.

He eventually felt that this only inflamed his opportunities to

be bullied.

Especially when the 300-pound freshmen began to get into his head saying that he would never amount to anything in sports.

In Matthew's sophomore year of high school, he started fresh. In this new school, no one knew the challenges that he had faced in the past, so this allowed him to feel a bit more confident. One day Matthew actually saw a quote on the internet which stated that wrestling is one of the only sports

where you can be a champion and your height or weight does not matter. Matthew decided to give this sport a try and instantly fell in love with it. He did not try to show off;

instead, he worked hard every day to be his best with a

consistent smile on his face. His hard work eventually paid off

and children at his school began to know him as the state

champ and the kid who broke the latest record. Matthew

gained confidence and realized that people actually looked up

to him. So, Matthew continues to wrestle. He has also been

able to have his college fully paid for. He found it ironic that

the last child that bullied him ended up serving him his meal

at a local fast-food

restaurant.

# Summary/ Key Takeaways: Step 5

- The first method of defense is to have an adult to get involved.

- A second way to get an adult involved would be for the offended party to approach a school authority themselves and express their concerns.

- A second method that has been effective in building a defense against bullies is for the offended party to assert themselves.

- One major assertion technique has been for individuals to defend themselves verbally.

- Another defense mechanism against bullies is of course- self-defense.

- It is also effective to just simply walk away.

- Sometimes the best defense against a bully is to understand them.

In the next chapter, you will learn how to share proof of a bullying issue.

# Step 6:

# Share the Proof!

## Step Six: Share the Proof

In **step six**, one must be wise in the method that they use to share the proof of their bullying situation. Once the individual has gathered proof of what has been occurring; it is wise to then share this proof with their authority figures. I

would suggest that the bullied individual start by sharing the proof with their guardian.

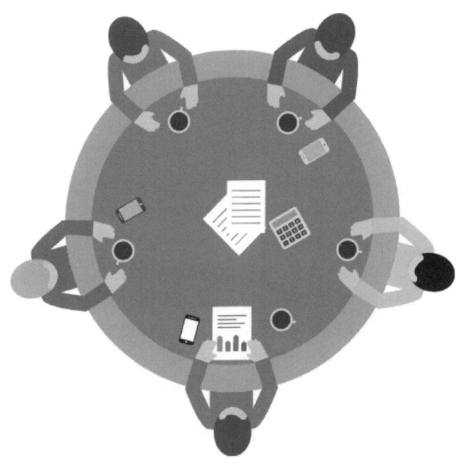

From there, they decide whether they want to take the proof to the teacher, principal, board of education, or the law. Many of us may have an opinion of what bullying is, but do not have a clear understanding of its textual meaning. Therefore, this documentation is necessary.

In the past, the law has not recognized bullying as a term on legal documents. This term was equated and replaced with words such as abuse, slander, battery, assault, etc. Thus, once bullying has hit a certain level…it is now a criminal act! When an individual presents proof of a harassment case; They must follow through rather than backing down and viewing themselves as a tattletale. To resolve this situation fear must be omitted, and individuals must speak out about the instances that occur.

# Summary/ Key Takeaways: Step 6

- Share proof with authority figures.

- Decide whether they want to take the proof to the teacher, principal, board of education, or the law.

- Sharing proof does not make you a tattletale.

- In the past, the law has not recognized bullying as a term on legal documents.

- In the next chapter, you will learn how to help other individuals walk in freedom.

# Step 7:

# Help Others Walk in Freedom

**Step Seven: Help Others to Walk in Freedom**

Once the individual has gained freedom from their situation of bullying, they can now go to **step seven** which is a mission to help others to be free from this unfortunate cycle. An individual needs to handle their bullying circumstance responsibly. This way, they can be a positive example to other victims that are going through similar issues. Thus, it is vital to take the tools learned here and apply them personally. This information must also be shared to empower others who feel trapped by despair.

The best way to lay aside your hurt is by helping others

 through theirs. Getting involved with bully awareness programs is a great way to get in touch with those that you may be able to

assist in overcoming bullying. Being a part of activities, events, and assisting financially would enable efforts of bully awareness to continue. Consider getting involved with such programs as the **Mikki High Bully No More! Project**.

www.MikkiHighBullyNoMore.org

This campaign was founded in 2011 and has assisted many individuals with being aware of the cause of and solution to the issue of bullying. One particularly effective tool has been the pledge that this non-profit has developed. This pledge is beneficial in providing a simple outline that will assist others in overcoming bullying.

# The Pledge:

1) **Be aware**. Be educated and informed. Know what bullying is and what it is not... Be able to recognize "bullying" when

you see it. Learn strategies to remove someone who is being bullied from the scene. Know what to say to safely deflate a bullying incident.

2) **Care**. Understand that you can help. Know what to do if you see bullying taking place in your school or community. Care enough to support with your words of encouragement, time, and resources to help spread the anti-bullying movement.

3) **Share**. Share information, protection, and encouragement. Teach others to accept the differences in others. If you are an adult, teach the youth around you how to respond properly to bullying, whether they be the victim or the bystander. Take this pledge on behalf of a school. Adopt a no-nonsense policy and offer an open discussion on bullying throughout the entire school year.

4) **Dare**. Dare to speak up, speak out, and *Stop Bullying Now*! Take preventative measures against bullying. Be proactive and empower your community with education. Dare to be a part of a growing movement to stomp out bullying.

**Me:**                **Pledge Card**

(I stand against bullying and raise awareness to the cause of and solution to bullying with Mikki High and the Mikki High Bully No More! Project.)

**Name**_____

**Date**_____
www.MikkiHighBullyNoMore.org

---

**Friend:**              **Pledge Card**
(I stand against bullying and raise awareness to the cause of and solution to bullying with Mikki High and the Mikki High Bully No More! Project.)

**Name**_____

**Date**_____
www.MikkiHighBullyNoMore.org

# Summary/ Key Takeaways: Step 7

- An individual needs to handle their bullying circumstance responsibly.

- Get involved with bully awareness programs.

- Join the **Mikki High Bully No More! Project** team in its efforts to stamp out bullying.

- Be Aware.

- Care.

- Share.

- Dare.

- Be determined to help others walk in the freedom of bullying in their own lives.

## Epilogue/ Conclusion

Many types of bullying have plagued our society; however, the information provided throughout this guide has been developed to be an awareness tool for those who need it. The steps that have been provided in this resource should be implemented as a means of assistance for those who have a desire to overcome the unfortunate situation of bullying. One should not hesitate to implement the following components. First, understand and accept their unique S.H.A.P.E. Second, gain a comprehension of what truly constitutes bullying. Thirdly, understand how to analyze the bullying that is being faced. Fourth, being capable of building complementary relationships.

Fifth, knowing various methods of defense. Sixth, having an understanding of how to share proof that pertains to bullying. Finally, step seven, which is developed to assist others in walking in freedom by overcoming their circumstances of bullying. As a final component of our conclusion, there will be a review of vital statistics as well as an addition of others that are deemed as important to be informed of.

Prior to doing this, I would like to extend an immense thank you to each individual that has taken the time to become aware of these seven steps to overcoming bullying. It means so much to have partners like you that are striving alongside me to make the world a better place. Remember that even though the world may not change overnight; we can get to a place of love... even if it is one person at a time!

# Facts & Stats (Part 1)

- Over 160,000 students refuse to go to school every day because they are afraid, they will be bullied.

- According to a SAFE survey, teens in grades 6-10, are the most likely to be involved in bullying activities.

- About 80% of students in high school have encountered bullying in some way online.

- About 56% of students have witnessed a bullying crime take place while at school.

- There are about 71% of students report bullying as an ongoing problem.

(Source: Olweus Research & www.MikkiHighBullyNoMore.org

# Facts & Stats (Part 2)

- There is a relationship between bullying or being bullied and other types of violence, including suicide, fighting and carrying weapons.

- About 42 percent of kids have been bullied while online with one in four being verbally attacked more than once.

- Over 80 percent of teens use a cell phone regularly, making it the most popular form of technology and a common medium for cyberbullying.

- About half of young people have experienced some form of cyberbullying, and 10 to 20 percent experience it regularly.

(Source: Olweus Research & www.MikkiHighBullyNoMore.org)

## Facts & Stats (Part 3)

- Mean, hurtful comments and spreading rumors are the most common type of cyberbullying.

- There are about 282,000 students that are reportedly attacked in high schools throughout the nation each month.

- Girls are at least as likely as boys to be cyberbullies or their victims.

- Boys are more likely to be threatened by cyberbullies than girls.

- Cyberbullying affects all races.

- Over half, about 56 percent, of all students have witnessed a bullying crime take place while at school.

(Source: Olweus Research & www.MikkiHighBullyNoMore.org)

## Facts & Stats (Part 4)

- A reported 15 percent of all students who do not show up for school report it to being out of fear of being bullied while at school.

- There is about 71 percent of students report bullying as an on-going problem.

- Along that same vein, about one out of every 10 students drop out or change schools because of repeated bullying.

- One out of every 20 students has seen a student with a gun at school.

(Source: Olweus Research & www.MikkiHighBullyNoMore.org)

## Facts & Stats (Part 5)

- Some of the top years for bullying include 4th through 8th graders in which 90 percent were reported as victims of some kind of bullying.

- Other recent bullying statistics reveal that 54 percent of students reported that witnessing physical abuse at home can lead to violence in school.

- Among students of all ages, homicide perpetrators were found to be twice as likely as homicide victims to have been bullied previously by their peers.

(Source: Olweus Research & www.MikkiHighBullyNoMore.org)

# About the Author

Tiffany "Mikki High" Hoffman (born April 25, 1995) is an author, motivational speaker, performance artist, actress, and television show hostess that strives to better humanity. After graduating as valedictorian from Interfaith Academy and starting college at age 16; She also began professionally speaking during the same year. It was at this time that she and her father organized The Mikki High Bully No More! Project® in response to personal tragedy and triumph in their own lives. She has a passion to see young children and teens live their lives free from abuse, fear, and oppression. Because of her heart, determination, and persistence, Mikki has received several medals of honor, awards, and recognitions.

Aside from graduating with a bachelor's degree in Business Administration with a concentration in finance and maintaining Dean's List status throughout her college years; She has received her Doctorate (ABA) from Interfaith University. Mikki has also been presented with the Tuskegee University Youth

Empowerment Summit Award, the You Make the Difference Award from IAMBK, and has been ordained as a Youth Minister by FOFMI. Mikki, like millions of other adolescents, was at one time bullied but found solace in writing music and playing the guitar. Now as a music recording artist and the national spokesperson for The Mikki High Bully No More! Project®, she is devoted to giving a voice to the thousands of students who live in silence because of bullying. With her concerts, rallies, movie nights, and public speaking events this artist sets the stage for student empowerment. She and her father launched www.MikkiHighBullyNoMore.org which provides free statistics, blogs, news, testimonials, and bully awareness tools internationally.

Being the spokesperson for The Mikki High Bully No More! Project®, Mikki has toured across the southeastern part of the United States visiting private and public schools, churches, community sponsored events, and shopping malls promoting bully awareness, education, and prevention. Through her website, television show, bully awareness app, bully no more petition, and bully awareness information hotline Mikki High reaches millions worldwide with the message of Hope and Love to those closely affected by

Through her public appearances and speaking

engagements, Mikki High is

instrumental in getting youth

and adults to understand that

bullying is a very serious

issue that has gone on far too

long and we all have a part to

make a difference. Mikki,

along with her team, faithfully set up kiosks throughout the

community to pass out literature on the topic of bullying.

This commitment has not only led many others to do the

same, but also allows the project to extend its range of

influence further. We are excited that young people will be

able to live productive lives in the absence of bullying in their

homes, schools, workplaces, and society altogether.

Mikki High is privileged for every opportunity she has been afforded to share her mission, music, and message to so many! She has been recognized for her work with The Mikki High Bully No More! Project® by several television networks, radio stations, newspapers, and community leaders and service organizations. Aside from Mikki being interviewed by reporters or on stage; she loves to spend time serving others and enjoying time with family and friends. During the next few years, her goal is to continue touring the country and encouraging others to take an active role in bully prevention, awareness, and education. She hopes that more people will join the movement with The Mikki High Bully No More! Project® and help stamp out bullying.

# Acknowledgments.

I would like to say thank you to everyone that has helped me in my journey to overcoming bullying.

A special thank you to my parents Dr. Ludie Lemont and Latricia Hoffman for always teaching and showing me the love of God. I know that without your support  and loving example; no goal accomplished would have been as easily achievable. I am so thankful to God for both of you and each of my siblings. Also, thank you to every partner that helps with this constant mission of bully awareness. My prayer is that this awareness guide that has been written from my heart is a key element in assisting those that have a desire to overcome bullying.

-Tiffany "Mikki High" Hoffman

# Motivational Moments (Part 1.)

*(These motivational moments are heartfelt words from bully awareness partners that are meant to encourage. Some words have been edited due to grammatical errors.)*

❖ "Don't let others stop you from being who you are. Don't let other children's opinions stop you from being who God made you to be."

*- Grace, Bully Awareness Partner*

❖ "This project has impacted my life in more ways than I can express! Thank you Mikki High and the Bully No More Team for all that you do to stamp out the huge problem of bullying!"

*– David, Bully Awareness Partner*

# Motivational Moments (Part 2.)

*(These motivational moments are heartfelt words from bully awareness partners that are meant to encourage. Some words have been edited due to grammatical errors.)*

❖ "I think bullying should stop!"

*-Shaleena, Bully Awareness Partner*

❖ "No matter what any person may say negatively to you or about you. Just know that you are somebody important."

*-Sarah, Bully Awareness Partner*

# Motivational Moments (Part 3.)

*(These motivational moments are heartfelt words from bully awareness partners that are meant to encourage. Some words have been edited due to grammatical errors.)*

❖ "…I was bullied, and I am here to tell you that you can make it! You are stronger than you think; when someone bullies you, it is just that they are not happy with their own life. Remember, everyone is strong. I am here to tell you that you can make it! I am living proof."

*-Tabatha, Bully Awareness Partner*

❖ "Stay encouraged…"

*-EJ, Bully Awareness Partner*

144

# Motivational Moments (Part 4.)

*(These motivational moments are heartfelt words from bully awareness partners that are meant to encourage. Some words have been edited due to grammatical errors.)*

❖ "BE YOURSELF"

> *-Jadyn, Bully Awareness Partner*

❖ "Everybody is perfect in their own way…"

> *-Anastasia, Bully Awareness Partner*

❖ "Stop bullying it is NOT right or nice."

> *-Dmitria, Bully Awareness Partner*

# Motivational Moments (Part 5.)

*(These motivational moments are heartfelt words from bully awareness partners that are meant to encourage. Some words have been edited due to grammatical errors.)*

❖ Walk away!

*-Chloe, Bully Awareness Partner*

❖ If you are ever bullied or see someone being bullied, do not be afraid to stand up for them!

*-Matthew, Bully Awareness Partner*

❖ Never let what other people say define you. You are great!

*-Krystyl, Bully Awareness Partner*

# Motivational Moments (Part 6.)

*(These motivational moments are heartfelt words from bully awareness partners that are meant to encourage. Some words have been edited due to grammatical errors.)*

❖ Do NOT ever think that you are the problem. Always know you make your path.

*-Danielle, Bully Awareness Partner*

❖ The person bullying you is just rude and bored. So just know that keep a straight face and walk.

*-Justin, Bully Awareness Partner*

❖ Hebrews 6:12

*-Kay, Bully Awareness Partner*

# Motivational Moments (Part 7.)

*(These motivational moments are heartfelt words from bully awareness partners that are meant to encourage. Some words have been edited due to grammatical errors.)*

❖ "I was bullied. I had so much mental, physical, and emotional pain that I was holding on to. The thing that freed me was forgiveness. I accepted God's forgiveness of everything that I had done wrong in my past and chose to trust Him to lead me in my future! This even helped me to let go of the pain that I was holding on to and forgive those that had bullied me. Oh yeah, here are some steps that I took. I hope that this helps you too!"

-*Michelle, Bully Awareness Partner*

# Motivational Moments (Part 8.)

1) Admit that you have done wrong in your past.

2) Repent of the wrong that you did.

3) Confess that Jesus Christ is Lord.

4) Believe God has raised His Son Jesus from the dead.

5.) Obey God's Word and His will for your life.

Romans 3:23 *(King James Version Bible)*

[23] For all have sinned and come short of the glory of God.

Romans 6:23

[23] For the wages of sin is death, but the gift of God is eternal life through Jesus Christ our Lord.

Romans 5:8

[8] But God commendeth his love toward us, in that, while we were yet sinners, Christ died for us.

Romans 10:9

[9] That if thou shalt confess with thy mouth the Lord Jesus, and shalt believe in thine heart that God hath raised him from the dead, thou shalt be saved.

# Motivational Moments (Part 7.)

*(These motivational moments are heartfelt words from bully awareness partners that are meant to encourage. Some words have been edited due to grammatical errors.)*

❖ Overcome all obstacles in your life!

*-Anthony, Bully Awareness Partner*

❖ You are loved!

*-Kityarra, Bully Awareness Partner*

❖ It gets better!

*-William, Bully Awareness Partner*

❖ "Keep your head high. You are strong."

*-Ivy, Bully Awareness Partner*

# Notes

# Notes

# Notes

# Notes

# Notes

# Notes

# Notes

_____

_____

_____

_____

_____

_____

_____

_____

_____

_____

_____

_____

# Bibliography

1769 King James Version of The Holy Bible (Authorized Version). Published 1769, public domain.

(2012). The Mikki High Bully No More! Project.

Olweus, D., & Limber, S. P. (2010). Olweus Research.

Made in the USA
Columbia, SC
29 November 2021

49943777R00093